The Future

Security in the Age of

Advanced Language Models

A Short Introduction by K.R. Stonebridge

The Future of Words:
Security in the Age of Advanced Language Models

ISBN: 9798877105386

Copyright © 2024 Brevity Books

Printed in the United States of America

Contents

Chapter 2:
The Security Landscape

Chapter 3:
Ethical Considerations

Chapter 4:
Mitigating Risks

Chapter 5:
The Future of AI in Language and Security

Conclusion:
Navigating a Secure Path Forward

Introduction: The Dawn of Advanced Language Models

The Evolution of Language Technology

The journey of language technology is a fascinating story of human ingenuity and technological advancement. It's a narrative that spans centuries, from the earliest forms of written communication to the complex algorithms powering today's advanced language models. This evolution has not only transformed how we interact with machines but also reshaped the landscape of communication, information processing, and even our understanding of language itself.

The origins of language technology can be traced back to the ancient civilizations that first developed writing systems. These early efforts in recording and transmitting language laid the foundational stone for the concept of encoding information. Fast forward to the 20th century, the invention of the computer brought a paradigm shift. The mid-1900s witnessed the first attempts at machine translation, a task that seemed almost insurmountable at the time. These initial forays, though rudimentary and often inaccurate, set the stage for the development of computational linguistics.

The advent of the internet and the digital age in the late 20th century catalyzed a significant leap in language technology. The explosion of digital text provided an unprecedented amount of data for analysis and processing. This era saw the development of basic language processing tools like spell checkers and grammar correction algorithms, which, while simple, were revolutionary in making written communication more efficient and accessible.

However, the real game-changer was the introduction of machine learning and, subsequently, deep learning techniques. Unlike their rule-based predecessors, these models didn't rely on hard-coded instructions but learned from data. This shift marked the beginning of a new era in language technology. Early machine learning models in natural language processing (NLP) focused on specific tasks like text classification or sentiment analysis. They were impressive but still limited by the amount and quality of the training data.

The breakthrough came with the development of large-scale language models, such as the GPT (Generative Pretrained Transformer) series. These models, trained on vast amounts of text, could generate coherent and contextually relevant text, perform language translation, answer questions, and even write creative content. Their ability to understand and generate human-like text was unparalleled, marking a significant milestone in the journey of language technology.

This evolution brought with it profound implications. Advanced language models opened new possibilities in fields like customer service, where chatbots could handle inquiries with increasing sophistication. In journalism, they assisted in drafting articles, especially for data-driven reporting. Even more impactful was their role in educational tools, providing personalized learning experiences and accessible language learning platforms.

But this progress was not without its challenges. The sophistication of these models raised concerns around misinformation, as they could generate plausible yet entirely fabricated content. Ethical considerations around the use of such technology became a paramount discussion, leading to a renewed focus on responsible AI development and deployment.

Looking ahead, the future of language technology seems boundless. The ongoing research aims not only to enhance the capabilities of these models but also to address their limitations and potential misuses. As we stand on the cusp of a new era in language technology, it is essential to reflect on this journey. Understanding the evolution of this field not only provides a context for current advancements but also guides us in navigating the ethical and practical challenges that lie ahead.

In summary, the evolution of language technology is a testament to human creativity and adaptability. From the first written symbols to sophisticated AI models, this journey highlights our enduring quest to enhance and refine communication. As we continue to innovate, it is crucial to balance the potential of these technologies with a mindful approach towards their impact on society and individual lives.

Defining Advanced Language Models

In the evolving world of artificial intelligence, advanced language models stand at the forefront, representing a remarkable intersection of linguistics, computer science, and artificial intelligence. These models, often referred to as the pinnacle of natural language processing (NLP), have transformed the way machines understand and generate human language. To appreciate their significance, it is crucial to delve into what these models are, how they function, and why they represent a significant leap in AI technology.

At their core, advanced language models are a type of artificial intelligence that processes, understands, and generates human language. They are built on the framework of machine learning, particularly deep learning, which allows them to learn from vast datasets of text. Unlike earlier models that relied on rule-based systems, these models use a probabilistic approach, learning patterns and nuances of language through exposure to large text corpora.

The architecture of these models is complex and often based on neural networks, specifically a type known as Transformer networks. This architecture, first introduced in a paper titled "Attention Is All You Need" in 2017, revolutionized NLP. The key innovation of Transformer models is their use of attention mechanisms, which allow the model to weigh the importance of different words in a sentence, giving context a central role in understanding language.

The most well-known example of an advanced language model is the Generative Pretrained Transformer (GPT) series developed by

OpenAI. These models are trained on diverse internet text and are capable of a wide range of language tasks. From writing essays to coding, GPT models have shown a remarkable ability to generate coherent and contextually relevant text. Their training involves unsupervised learning, where the model is exposed to text without specific instructions, allowing it to learn the intricacies of language independently.

The significance of these models lies in their versatility and efficiency. They are not programmed for a specific language task but can adapt to various tasks with minimal task-specific training. This flexibility marks a departure from earlier models that were typically designed for narrow applications. Moreover, advanced language models have an unprecedented ability to generate human-like text, opening new possibilities in fields such as content creation, customer service, and even creative writing.

However, the power of these models also brings challenges. The quality of their output depends heavily on the training data, which can embed biases and inaccuracies if not carefully curated. Additionally, their ability to generate plausible text raises concerns about misinformation and the potential for misuse in creating false narratives.

Despite these challenges, the potential applications of advanced language models are vast. In healthcare, they can assist in processing patient data and generating medical reports. In education, they offer tools for personalized learning and language tutoring. In business, they can automate customer interactions and analyze market trends. The possibilities are as varied as the tasks that involve language.

As we continue to integrate these models into various aspects of our lives, it is essential to approach their development and deployment responsibly. This involves addressing ethical concerns, ensuring data privacy, and mitigating biases in training data. The future of advanced language models is not just about technological advancement but also about navigating the societal and ethical implications of such powerful tools.

In conclusion, advanced language models represent a significant milestone in the journey of artificial intelligence. They embody the culmination of decades of research in NLP and machine learning, offering a glimpse into a future where machines can understand and interact in human language with unprecedented sophistication. As we harness their potential, it is crucial to do so with a mindful approach, ensuring that these models serve the greater good and contribute positively to society.

The Broad Impact on Society and Security

The advent and proliferation of advanced language models have far-reaching implications, deeply influencing various facets of society and posing new challenges in the domain of security. The impact of these sophisticated AI systems is not just limited to technological advancements; it profoundly affects social interactions, information dissemination, privacy, and even the very fabric of security as we know it.

Transforming Communication and Information Accessibility

Advanced language models have revolutionized communication, making it more seamless and inclusive. These AI systems can translate languages with remarkable accuracy, bridging communication gaps across cultures and geographies. This capability enhances global connectivity, fostering cross-cultural understanding and collaboration. Moreover, they have significantly democratized information accessibility. People with disabilities, such as those with visual impairments or language processing disorders, can now access information more easily through AI-driven tools that convert text to speech or simplify complex language.

However, the ease of accessing and generating information also comes with challenges. The ability of these models to create convincing and coherent text has led to concerns about the generation of fake news and the spread of misinformation. The ease with which convincing articles, reports, and even deepfake videos can be produced poses a threat to the integrity of information, potentially swaying public opinion, influencing elections, and inciting social unrest.

Impact on Education and Workforce

In education, advanced language models serve as powerful tools, providing personalized learning experiences and aiding in research. They can offer students tailored educational content and assist teachers in grading and providing feedback. However, this also raises concerns about academic integrity, as these tools can be used to generate essays and assignments, making it challenging to assess a student's actual understanding and skills.

The workforce landscape is also being reshaped by these AI models. Many tasks that previously required human expertise, such as customer service, content creation, and even certain aspects of programming, can now be automated or assisted by AI, leading to increased efficiency. This shift prompts a reevaluation of job roles and the skills required in the workforce, emphasizing adaptability and the ability to work alongside AI systems.

Privacy and Data Security

The operation of advanced language models hinges on large datasets, often collected from public and private sources. This raises significant privacy concerns. The data used to train these models may contain sensitive information, and if not handled properly, there is a risk of data breaches and misuse. Ensuring the privacy and security of data used in training and operating these models is paramount.

Moreover, the capability of these models to generate realistic and personalized content opens avenues for sophisticated phishing attacks and scams. Personalized and convincing messages generated by AI can be used to deceive individuals, potentially leading to identity theft, financial fraud, and the spread of malware.

Shaping Policies and Regulations

The broad impact of advanced language models necessitates thoughtful consideration in policy and regulation. Governments and international bodies face the challenge of balancing innovation with ethical considerations and security. Policies need to address issues like data privacy, misinformation, AI accountability, and the ethical use of AI. Additionally, there's a growing need for international cooperation to manage the global implications of these technologies, from cybersecurity to information warfare.

Conclusion

Advanced language models, with their vast capabilities, are reshaping society and the landscape of security in profound ways. While they offer remarkable benefits in communication, education, and efficiency, they also introduce complex challenges that need to be managed with a balanced approach. As we continue to integrate these AI systems into various sectors, it is crucial to foster an environment of responsible AI development, ethical use, and robust security measures. The future will likely see a continued evolution of these technologies, and our response to these challenges will shape the impact of AI on society and security in the coming decades.

Chapter 1: Understanding Language Models

The Mechanics of Language AI

In the realm of artificial intelligence, language models stand as a pinnacle of complexity and sophistication. Understanding the mechanics behind these models is essential for grasping their capabilities and limitations. This exploration into the inner workings of language AI unveils a world where computer science, linguistics, and mathematics intersect, resulting in the powerful tools we see today.

Foundations of Natural Language Processing (NLP)

At the core of language AI is natural language processing (NLP), a field of computer science and linguistics focused on the interaction between computers and human languages. NLP aims to enable computers to understand, interpret, and generate human language in a valuable and meaningful way. The fundamental challenge of NLP lies in the complexity and nuance of human language, including its rules, slang, idioms, and the context within which it is used.

To tackle these challenges, early NLP systems relied on rule-based methods, where linguists manually crafted rules for language processing. These systems were effective for specific, limited tasks but lacked the flexibility and scalability needed for more complex language understanding.

The Rise of Machine Learning in NLP

The advent of machine learning, especially deep learning, marked a significant shift in NLP. Instead of relying on hardcoded rules, these models learn to process language by being trained on large datasets. The training involves feeding the model examples of language use, allowing it to adjust its internal parameters to better predict or generate text.

The backbone of modern NLP models is the neural network, particularly a variant known as recurrent neural networks (RNNs). These networks are adept at processing sequences of data, like sentences, and can maintain a form of memory, essential for understanding context. However, RNNs have limitations, particularly in handling long-range dependencies in text.

Breakthrough with Transformer Models

The introduction of the Transformer model, as seen in models like Google's BERT and OpenAI's GPT series, represents a significant breakthrough in NLP. Unlike RNNs, Transformers use an attention mechanism that allows the model to weigh and focus on different parts of the input sequence differently. This ability to focus on relevant parts of the input makes Transformers particularly effective at understanding context and generating coherent, contextually relevant text.

The architecture of Transformer models consists of layers of self-attention and feedforward neural networks. The self-attention mechanism enables the model to evaluate the importance of all words in a sentence, providing a rich understanding of context. This architectural advancement allows for more parallelization during training, leading to larger and more powerful models.

Training and Fine-Tuning

Training these models involves two main phases: pre-training and fine-tuning. During pre-training, the model is exposed to a vast corpus of text, learning the general patterns and structures of the language. This phase does not require labeled data, making it an example of unsupervised learning. Once pre-trained, the model can be fine-tuned for specific tasks, like translation, question-answering, or text generation, using smaller, task-specific datasets.

The size and quality of the training data are crucial. Models trained on more diverse and extensive text corpora tend to perform better. However, this also raises concerns about biases in the training data, which can lead to biased outputs.

Challenges and Future Directions

Despite their advancements, language AI models face challenges. They require vast computational resources for training, raising concerns about environmental impact and accessibility. Additionally, these models often lack true understanding, sometimes generating plausible but nonsensical or factually incorrect text. Addressing these challenges involves ongoing research in making models more efficient, interpretable, and capable of more nuanced understanding.

Conclusion

The mechanics of language AI represent a fascinating blend of technical ingenuity and linguistic insight. From the basic principles of NLP to the sophisticated architecture of Transformer models, the journey of language AI is one of continuous innovation and advancement. As we look towards the future, the potential for these models to further revolutionize how we interact with technology and process information is immense, promising a landscape where AI aids in breaking down language barriers and enhancing global communication.

Evolution from Simple Algorithms to Complex Models

The field of language technology has witnessed a remarkable evolution, transitioning from simple algorithms to today's highly complex models. This journey is not just a tale of technological advancement but also a reflection of our deepening understanding of language and computation. Tracing this evolution provides insight into how language models have become an integral part of our digital landscape.

The Early Days: Rule-Based Systems

The earliest attempts at language processing in computers were rule-based systems. These systems, which emerged in the mid-20th century, were built on sets of handcrafted rules formulated by linguists. They attempted to encode the grammar and syntax of language into a format that computers could understand and process. These early systems were adept at handling structured, predictable text but struggled with the nuances and variability of natural language. Their most significant limitation was the lack of scalability and flexibility, as they could not easily adapt to new languages or unexpected language use.

The Advent of Statistical Methods

The limitations of rule-based systems led to the adoption of statistical methods in language processing. This shift, which started in the late 1980s and gained momentum in the 1990s, was fueled by the increasing availability of digital text data and advancements in computing power. Statistical NLP focused on analyzing language data to find patterns and make predictions. Techniques like n-gram models, which predicted the probability of a word based on its preceding words, were foundational in this era. These methods were more flexible and scalable than rule-based systems, allowing for more effective processing of natural language.

The Rise of Machine Learning

The next significant leap in language technology came with the integration of machine learning, particularly in the early 2000s. Machine learning models, trained on large datasets, could learn language patterns without explicit programming. This approach marked a departure from relying solely on linguistic rules or statistical probabilities. Techniques like decision trees, support vector machines, and later, neural networks, started to redefine what was possible in NLP. These models excelled at tasks like text classification, sentiment analysis, and named entity recognition, offering a more nuanced understanding of language.

Breakthrough with Deep Learning

The introduction of deep learning, a subset of machine learning involving layered neural networks, revolutionized NLP. Deep learning models, especially recurrent neural networks (RNNs) and later, long short-term memory networks (LSTMs), were particularly well-suited for handling sequential data like text. They could remember information over long sequences, making them effective for tasks requiring context understanding, like machine translation.

The Era of Transformer Models

The current pinnacle of language technology is the era of Transformer models, initiated by the introduction of models like Google's BERT and OpenAI's GPT. These models use a unique architecture that eschews recurrence in favor of attention mechanisms, allowing them to process entire sequences of text simultaneously. This architecture has led to significant improvements in a variety of NLP tasks and has enabled the training of even larger and more powerful models. Transformers have set new standards for what's possible in language understanding and generation, performing tasks with a level of sophistication that was previously unattainable.

The Impact of Large-Scale Language Models

The most recent and perhaps the most transformative development in language technology has been the advent of large-scale language models like GPT-4. These models are trained on vast corpora of text data, encompassing a wide range of topics, styles, and languages. Their size and the amount of data they are trained on allow them to generate text that is remarkably coherent and contextually relevant. They represent a quantum leap in AI's ability to understand and generate human language, with applications ranging from writing assistance to conversational AI.

Challenges and Future Directions

Despite the incredible progress, the evolution from simple algorithms to complex models presents new challenges. These include ethical concerns, such as bias in AI models and the potential for misuse, and technical challenges, like the interpretability of model decisions and the environmental impact of training large models. Addressing these challenges is critical as we continue to advance in the field of language technology.

Conclusion

The evolution of language technology from simple algorithms to complex models is a testament to the remarkable progress in AI and computational linguistics. It highlights a journey from rigid, rule-based systems to flexible, learning-based models that can understand and generate human language with increasing sophistication. As we look to the future, the potential for further advancements in language technology is vast, promising to reshape our interaction with technology and further blur the lines between human and machine communication.

Real-World Applications and Implications

The development of advanced language models has opened up a myriad of applications that are transforming various sectors of society. From enhancing communication to revolutionizing industries, the impact of these AI-driven tools is profound and far-reaching. This section delves into the real-world applications of language models and their broader implications.

Revolutionizing Communication

One of the most immediate applications of language models is in enhancing and simplifying communication. AI-driven translation services have become remarkably accurate, breaking down language barriers and fostering global connectivity. Chatbots and virtual assistants, powered by sophisticated language models, are providing customer support, personalized assistance, and even companionship to users, reshaping the dynamics of customer service and personal interaction.

Impact on Media and Content Creation

In the realm of media and content creation, language models are playing a pivotal role. They assist in generating news articles, creative writing, and even scripting for movies and games. AI-generated content is not only efficient but can also be tailored to specific audiences or formats, making content creation more accessible and diversified. However, this also raises concerns about authenticity and the potential loss of human touch in creative endeavors.

Enhancing Educational Tools

Education is another sector witnessing a transformative impact due to language models. These AI systems offer personalized learning experiences, language tutoring, and assistance in writing and research. They make education more accessible and tailored to individual needs. However, this also presents challenges in ensuring academic integrity and the skill development of students.

Advancements in Healthcare

Language models are significantly contributing to healthcare by processing patient data, assisting in diagnostics, and even helping in mental health therapy. They can analyze patient histories, research, and reports, providing valuable insights for healthcare professionals. This application has the potential to revolutionize medical diagnostics and patient care, though it also necessitates careful consideration of privacy and ethical implications.

Transforming Business Operations

In the business sector, advanced language models are utilized for market analysis, customer insights, and automating routine tasks like email responses and document processing. This automation increases efficiency and allows businesses to focus on more strategic tasks. However, it also prompts a reevaluation of job roles and the skills required in the workforce.

Legal and Ethical Implications

The use of language models in legal research and document review is another growing application. These models can analyze legal documents, identify relevant cases, and even suggest legal strategies. While this enhances the efficiency of legal processes, it also raises questions about the role of AI in decision-making processes that have significant legal consequences.

Enhancing Accessibility

Language models significantly contribute to making information more accessible, especially for people with disabilities. Text-to-speech and speech-to-text functionalities are vital tools for individuals with visual or hearing impairments, enhancing their ability to communicate and access information.

Challenges and Ethical Considerations

The widespread application of language models is not without challenges. Issues such as data privacy, the potential for bias in AI models, and the ethical use of these technologies are at the forefront of discussions. As these models become more integrated into our daily lives, ensuring they are used responsibly and ethically is paramount.

Societal Impact

The societal impact of language models is profound. They are reshaping how we communicate, access information, and perform various tasks. However, this also leads to concerns about job displacement due to automation and the need for new skill sets to work alongside AI. Moreover, the potential for these models to be used in spreading misinformation and manipulating public opinion is a significant concern that needs to be addressed.

Future Directions

As we look to the future, the applications of language models are expected to grow and diversify. The ongoing development in AI will likely lead to more sophisticated and specialized uses, further transforming industries and societal functions. However, this progress also necessitates a concurrent focus on developing ethical guidelines, regulatory frameworks, and strategies to manage the challenges posed by these powerful technologies.

Conclusion

The real-world applications of advanced language models are vast and varied, touching nearly every aspect of modern life. From transforming industries to reshaping societal interactions, the implications of these AI-driven tools are monumental. As we continue to harness their potential, a balanced approach that considers both the benefits and challenges is essential to ensure these technologies contribute positively to society.

Chapter 2: The Security Landscape

Cybersecurity in the Age of AI

In an era where digital interconnectivity is ubiquitous, the advent of advanced artificial intelligence, especially sophisticated language models, has significantly transformed the landscape of cybersecurity. This transformation is not unidirectional; while AI offers enhanced tools for security, it also introduces novel vulnerabilities. Understanding these dynamics is crucial in navigating the digital world safely.

AI-Enhanced Security Systems

One of the most prominent applications of AI in cybersecurity is the enhancement of security systems. AI algorithms, particularly those based on machine learning, are adept at analyzing patterns and detecting anomalies. This capability is leveraged in identifying potential security threats, such as unusual network traffic, which could signify a cyberattack. AI systems can process vast amounts of data at a speed unattainable by human analysts, enabling real-time threat detection and response.

Furthermore, language models have revolutionized the field of phishing detection. By analyzing the text in emails and online communications, these models can identify potential phishing attempts more effectively than traditional methods. Their ability to understand the context and subtle cues in language makes them powerful tools in combating one of the most common cyber threats.

The Double-Edged Sword of AI in Cybersecurity

However, the integration of AI into cybersecurity is a double-edged sword. The same capabilities that make AI systems effective in enhancing security can also be exploited for malicious purposes. AI-driven attacks are a growing concern in cybersecurity circles. These attacks are more sophisticated, harder to detect, and can adapt in real-time to security measures.

One area of concern is the use of AI in creating sophisticated social engineering attacks. Advanced language models can generate convincing phishing emails or fraudulent communications that are much more difficult for individuals to identify as malicious. This increased sophistication in social engineering poses a significant challenge to existing security measures, which often rely on users' ability to spot inconsistencies or suspicious elements in messages.

AI in Malware and Exploit Development

AI technologies are also being used in the development of malware and exploits. AI algorithms can analyze software code to identify vulnerabilities that can be exploited. While this capability can be used for legitimate purposes, such as identifying and patching vulnerabilities, it also means that attackers can use AI to develop more effective malware or to identify new attack vectors.

Moreover, AI can be used to automate the customization of malware for specific targets, making traditional antivirus software less effective. The malware can adapt to the security environment of the target, modifying its behavior to avoid detection.

The Arms Race in Cybersecurity

The evolving landscape has led to an arms race between cyber attackers and defenders. As security systems become more sophisticated with AI, attackers are also leveraging AI to breach these systems. This dynamic necessitates a continuous effort in cybersecurity research and development to stay ahead of threats.

Ethical and Privacy Concerns

The use of AI in cybersecurity also raises ethical and privacy concerns. The extensive data collection and analysis required for AI-driven security systems can intrude on individual privacy. There is a delicate balance to be maintained between effective security measures and the protection of personal privacy.

The Role of Regulations and Policies

In response to these challenges, there is a growing need for regulations and policies specifically addressing the use of AI in cybersecurity. This includes guidelines on ethical AI development, data privacy, and standards for AI-driven security solutions. International collaboration is also crucial, as cybersecurity threats often transcend national boundaries.

Preparing for the Future

As AI continues to advance, staying prepared for future cybersecurity challenges is imperative. This preparation involves not just technological advancements but also training the workforce in AI-related security skills, raising public awareness about AI-driven threats, and developing robust legal frameworks to manage these issues.

Conclusion

Cybersecurity in the age of AI presents a complex landscape of enhanced defensive capabilities and emerging threats. The integration of AI into cybersecurity solutions offers significant advantages in threat detection and response. However, it also introduces new vulnerabilities and ethical considerations. Navigating this landscape requires a multi-faceted approach, combining technological innovation, skilled human expertise, ethical considerations, and collaborative international efforts. As AI technologies continue to evolve, so too must our strategies for maintaining digital security and privacy.

Potential Threats Posed by Language Models

The emergence of advanced language models in the field of artificial intelligence has not only brought about groundbreaking applications but also introduced a spectrum of potential threats. These risks, ranging from misinformation to privacy breaches, highlight the dual-use nature of this technology. Understanding these threats is crucial for developing effective strategies to mitigate them.

Misinformation and Propaganda

One of the most significant threats posed by advanced language models is their ability to generate convincing and coherent text. This ability can be exploited to produce large volumes of misinformation and propaganda at scale. Unlike traditional methods of creating false information, which require significant human effort, AI models can generate plausible-sounding narratives quickly and efficiently. This poses a substantial challenge in maintaining the integrity of information online and combating the spread of fake news.

Phishing and Social Engineering Attacks

Language models can be used to craft highly sophisticated phishing emails and execute social engineering attacks. By analyzing and mimicking the writing style of individuals or organizations, these AI systems can create personalized and convincing messages. Such messages are more likely to deceive recipients, leading to increased risks of identity theft, financial fraud, and access to sensitive information.

Privacy Concerns

Advanced language models, particularly those trained on vast datasets that include public and private information, pose significant privacy concerns. There's a risk that these models could inadvertently leak sensitive information embedded in their training data. Additionally, when used in applications like predictive text or virtual assistants, they could potentially expose personal details of users' conversations or preferences.

Manipulation and Behavioral Influence

The persuasive power of language models can be misused to manipulate public opinion and influence behavior. This is particularly concerning in the context of political campaigns, advertising, and propaganda. The ability of AI to analyze and generate content that resonates with specific demographics or individuals can lead to targeted manipulation, raising ethical concerns about autonomy and consent.

Automated Content Generation

While the ability of AI models to generate content can be beneficial, it also presents the risk of automated disinformation campaigns. These campaigns can flood social media platforms and the internet with misleading or false information, overwhelming efforts to fact-check and verify the authenticity of content.

Exploitation in Cyberattacks

Language models can be employed to enhance the sophistication of cyberattacks. For example, they can be used to write convincing phishing scripts, automate social engineering tactics, or even assist in coding more advanced malware. The adaptability and learning capabilities of these models make them potent tools in the hands of malicious actors.

Legal and Ethical Challenges

The deployment of language models in sensitive areas such as law enforcement, judiciary, or healthcare raises legal and ethical challenges. Their use in decision-making processes that can significantly impact people's lives necessitates careful consideration of the models' fairness, transparency, and accountability.

The Arms Race in AI

The development of advanced language models has initiated a sort of arms race in AI capabilities. As these models become more powerful, there is a concurrent race to develop countermeasures. This includes developing AI systems capable of detecting AI-generated content, leading to an ongoing cycle of advancement and counter-advancement.

Preparing for an AI-Driven Future

Given the potential threats posed by advanced language models, it is imperative to develop robust strategies to mitigate these risks. This includes investing in AI literacy and awareness, developing ethical guidelines for AI development and deployment, and implementing effective regulatory frameworks. Collaboration among tech companies, governments, and international bodies is crucial in addressing these global challenges.

Conclusion

Advanced language models, while a testament to human ingenuity in AI development, come with significant potential threats that need to be carefully managed. The risks of misinformation, privacy breaches, and manipulation are real and present challenges in an increasingly AI-driven world. Addressing these threats requires a multi-faceted approach, combining technological, ethical, legal, and educational strategies to ensure that the benefits of AI are harnessed responsibly and safely.

Case Studies: Security Breaches and AI

The integration of advanced AI into various sectors has not only brought about efficiency and innovation but also introduced new vulnerabilities in cybersecurity. Examining real-world case studies of security breaches involving AI, particularly language models, offers valuable insights into the nature of these threats and how they can be mitigated.

Case Study 1: AI-Powered Phishing Attacks

One notable instance of an AI-related security breach involved the use of a language model in a sophisticated phishing operation. The attackers used an AI system to analyze and mimic the communication styles of specific individuals in a corporation. By doing so, they crafted highly convincing phishing emails that successfully bypassed traditional email filters and tricked recipients into divulging sensitive information. This case highlighted the advanced capabilities of AI in mimicking human communication, underscoring the need for more AI-aware security measures and training for personnel.

Case Study 2: Deepfake Technology in Social Engineering

Another significant case involved the use of deepfake technology, a branch of AI that creates realistic audio and video forgeries. In this instance, fraudsters used a deepfake audio clip of a CEO's voice to instruct a subordinate to transfer a large sum of money to an external account. The voice was convincing enough to deceive the employee, leading to substantial financial loss. This incident underscored the potential of AI to create highly realistic forgeries, posing a threat to personal and corporate security.

Case Study 3: Automated Malware Generation

A more technically sophisticated breach involved the use of AI in creating and optimizing malware. In this case, the attackers used a machine learning algorithm to analyze security systems and generate malware capable of evading detection. The AI system continuously adapted the malware based on feedback, making it exceptionally resilient to traditional antivirus solutions. This breach demonstrated how AI could be utilized to automate and enhance the development of malicious software, challenging existing cybersecurity defenses.

Case Study 4: Data Breach Through Predictive Text

A less obvious but equally concerning breach involved a language model used in a predictive text application. The AI system inadvertently suggested sensitive information, including passwords and confidential data, which it had learned from previous user inputs. This incident revealed a significant privacy risk associated with training AI on sensitive data and highlighted the need for robust data handling and privacy protection measures in AI systems.

Lessons Learned from These Breaches

1. **Enhanced AI Security Measures**: These cases illustrate the need for more sophisticated security systems that can detect and counter AI-powered threats. This includes the development of AI systems capable of identifying deepfakes, phishing attempts, and advanced malware.

2. **Awareness and Training**: Raising awareness about AI-related threats and training employees to recognize and respond to such threats is crucial. This involves understanding the capabilities of AI in generating convincing forgeries and deceptive content.

3. **Regulatory and Ethical Frameworks**: The incidents underscore the importance of establishing regulatory and ethical frameworks governing the use of AI. This includes guidelines for responsible AI development and measures to prevent its misuse.

4. **Collaboration and Information Sharing**: Effective response to AI-driven threats requires collaboration between organizations, cybersecurity experts, and government agencies. Sharing information about threats and best practices can help in developing collective defense strategies.

5. **Investing in AI Research for Defense**: Investing in AI research focused on security applications is essential to stay ahead of AI-driven threats. This includes developing AI systems that can adapt to evolving threats and protect against AI-generated attacks.

Conclusion

The case studies of security breaches involving AI highlight the dual-use nature of advanced language models and AI technologies. While they offer significant benefits, they also introduce new and complex security challenges. Addressing these challenges requires a multifaceted approach, combining technological solutions, regulatory frameworks, awareness and training programs, and collaborative efforts across sectors. As AI continues to advance, staying vigilant and adaptive in cybersecurity strategies will be key to safeguarding against these evolving threats.

Chapter 3:
Ethical Considerations

Ethical Use of Language Models

The rise of advanced language models in various sectors has not only brought technological advancements but also raised significant ethical questions. The ethical use of these AI tools is a subject of crucial importance, involving the responsibilities and challenges faced by developers, users, and policymakers.

Understanding the Ethical Implications

Language models, with their ability to understand, interpret, and generate human-like text, hold immense power. This power, if misused, can lead to issues like the spread of misinformation, privacy violations, and reinforcement of biases. The ethical use of language models, therefore, involves understanding and addressing these potential negative impacts.

Transparency and Accountability

A key aspect of the ethical use of language models is transparency in their development and deployment. Users should be aware of how these models work, the nature of the data they were trained on, and their limitations. This transparency is crucial in building trust and ensuring accountability, especially when these models make errors or when their use leads to unintended consequences.

Addressing Bias and Fairness

Language models can inadvertently perpetuate and amplify biases present in their training data. This can lead to unfair or discriminatory outcomes when these models are used in decision-making processes. Ethically using these models involves actively working to identify and mitigate biases, ensuring fairness in AI-generated content and decisions.

Respecting Privacy and Consent

The vast datasets used to train language models often contain personal information. Ethically using these models means respecting the privacy of individuals and ensuring that data is used with consent and in compliance with data protection laws. This is particularly important in applications like personalized marketing, healthcare, or any field where sensitive information is involved.

Ensuring Safety and Security

The potential misuse of language models for malicious purposes like phishing, fraud, or generating harmful content poses significant ethical challenges. Ensuring the safety and security of AI systems is a crucial aspect of their ethical use. This involves implementing safeguards to prevent misuse and developing strategies to quickly address any harmful outcomes that may arise.

Role of Developers and Companies

The responsibility for the ethical use of language models begins with their developers and the companies behind them. This involves ethical AI design principles, thorough testing for biases, transparency about capabilities and limitations, and a commitment to ongoing monitoring and improvement of these systems.

User Responsibility

Users of language models, whether individuals, businesses, or organizations, also bear responsibility for their ethical use. This includes being informed about the nature and limitations of the AI tools they are using, employing them in a manner that respects privacy and fairness, and being vigilant about potential misuse.

Policymaking and Regulation

Governments and regulatory bodies play a crucial role in ensuring the ethical use of language models. This involves creating policies and regulations that promote ethical AI development and use, protecting individuals' rights, and providing guidelines for addressing ethical dilemmas in AI applications.

The Importance of Public Discourse

Ethical considerations around language models should be a part of public discourse. Open discussions involving experts, policymakers, and the general public can help in understanding the societal implications of these technologies and in shaping norms and policies that govern their use.

Preparing for Future Challenges

As language models continue to evolve and become more integrated into various aspects of life, preparing for future ethical challenges is essential. This involves continuous research into the societal impacts of AI, development of new ethical frameworks as technology advances, and fostering a culture of responsibility among all stakeholders.

Conclusion

The ethical use of language models is a multifaceted issue that requires the involvement of developers, users, and policymakers. It is about creating a balance between leveraging the benefits of these powerful AI tools and mitigating their potential harms. As we advance further into an AI-driven era, the ethical considerations surrounding these technologies will become increasingly important, necessitating a collaborative and proactive approach to ensure they benefit society as a whole.

Balancing Innovation with Privacy

In the age of advanced language models, the intersection of innovation and privacy has become a critical area of focus. As these AI-driven technologies evolve, they bring unparalleled benefits but also pose significant challenges to privacy. Striking a balance between embracing innovation and safeguarding privacy is a complex yet essential task.

The Privacy Challenges Posed by AI

Advanced language models, by their nature, require access to vast amounts of data to learn and function effectively. This data often includes sensitive personal information, raising concerns about privacy breaches. The ability of these models to generate, predict, and even mimic human language and behavior can also lead to inadvertent exposure of personal data or be used to infer private information.

The Need for Data Protection

Protecting data in the age of AI involves more than just securing information from unauthorized access. It also means ensuring that data used to train and operate language models is handled responsibly. This includes considerations like data minimization, where only the necessary data is collected, and anonymization, where personal identifiers are removed.

Consent and Transparency

Obtaining explicit consent from individuals before using their data for AI applications is a fundamental aspect of balancing privacy with innovation. Users should be made aware of how their data will be used, the purpose of the AI systems, and any potential risks involved. Transparency in AI operations, including how models are trained and the nature of the data they use, is crucial in building trust and ensuring ethical use.

Ethical AI Development

Developers of language models have a significant responsibility in ensuring that their creations do not infringe on individual privacy. This involves ethical AI development practices, such as incorporating privacy considerations into the design process, regularly auditing models for privacy risks, and implementing mechanisms to prevent the misuse of personal data.

Regulatory Frameworks and Policies

Effective regulatory frameworks and policies are essential in maintaining the balance between innovation and privacy. Governments and regulatory bodies need to establish clear guidelines and standards for AI development and use, particularly regarding data protection. These regulations should be flexible enough to adapt to the rapidly evolving AI landscape while robust enough to protect individual privacy.

The Role of Privacy-Enhancing Technologies

Privacy-enhancing technologies (PETs) play a critical role in balancing innovation with privacy. These technologies, such as differential privacy and homomorphic encryption, enable the use of data in AI applications while minimizing the risk of exposing personal information. Investing in and adopting these technologies is crucial for organizations leveraging language models.

User Empowerment

Empowering users with control over their data is a key strategy in maintaining privacy. This includes providing options for users to opt-out of data collection, access the data collected about them, and request deletion of their data. User empowerment not only respects individual privacy rights but also fosters a more trusting relationship between users and AI applications.

Balancing Innovation and Privacy in Practice

Implementing a balanced approach to innovation and privacy requires practical strategies. For organizations using language models, this could involve conducting privacy impact assessments, training employees on data protection best practices, and establishing clear data governance policies.

Preparing for Future Challenges

As language models continue to advance, new privacy challenges will inevitably arise. Preparing for these future challenges involves continuous monitoring of the AI landscape, investing in research on privacy-preserving AI techniques, and fostering a culture of privacy awareness within the AI community.

Conclusion

Balancing the innovation offered by advanced language models with the need to protect privacy is a nuanced and ongoing process. It requires a collaborative effort involving developers, users, policymakers, and regulatory bodies. By implementing robust privacy measures, fostering transparency, and adhering to ethical standards, we can harness the benefits of AI while respecting and protecting individual privacy. As AI technologies evolve, this balance will remain a cornerstone of responsible and sustainable AI development and deployment.

Regulations and Compliance in a Digital Era

The rapid advancement of language models and AI technologies in the digital era has necessitated a reevaluation of regulatory frameworks and compliance measures. These technologies, while offering immense benefits, also pose unique challenges that existing laws may not adequately address. This section explores the evolving landscape of regulations and compliance in the context of advanced language models.

The Need for Updated Regulations

Traditional legal frameworks often struggle to keep pace with the rapid development of technology. The unique capabilities and potential risks associated with language models and AI require a fresh approach to regulation. This includes considerations of privacy, data protection, intellectual property, and ethical use of AI. Regulations need to be updated to reflect the realities of AI-driven technologies, ensuring they are used responsibly and safely.

Balancing Innovation and Protection

A key challenge in developing regulations for AI and language models is balancing the need to protect the public and the environment with the need to foster innovation. Overly stringent regulations could stifle technological advancement and hinder the benefits AI can bring. Conversely, lax regulations could lead to misuse of AI, privacy violations, and other risks. Striking this balance requires careful consideration and input from various stakeholders, including technologists, legal experts, policymakers, and the public.

Global and Local Regulatory Approaches

The global nature of AI technology and the digital economy poses another challenge for regulation. Different countries may have varying approaches to privacy, data protection, and AI governance. This diversity can lead to complications for companies operating internationally. There is a growing need for international cooperation and harmonization of AI regulations to ensure consistent standards while respecting local laws and cultural differences.

Data Protection and Privacy Laws

Data is at the heart of AI and language models. Effective regulations need to address how data is collected, used, and protected. This includes ensuring informed consent for data collection, establishing clear guidelines for data usage, and implementing robust measures to protect personal and sensitive information. GDPR in the European Union is an example of comprehensive data protection legislation that has implications for AI development and deployment.

Ethical Guidelines and AI Governance

Beyond legal regulations, ethical guidelines play a crucial role in the governance of AI. These guidelines help bridge the gap between existing laws and the fast-evolving nature of AI technologies. They can provide a framework for responsible AI development, focusing on issues like fairness, transparency, accountability, and ensuring AI benefits society as a whole.

Compliance Challenges for Organizations

Organizations employing AI and language models face significant compliance challenges. They need to navigate a complex web of regulations that may vary by region and industry. Ensuring compliance requires not only a thorough understanding of relevant laws but also implementing internal policies and practices that align with these regulations.

The Role of AI in Regulatory Compliance

Interestingly, AI itself can be a tool to assist with regulatory compliance. AI systems can help organizations monitor and analyze their operations, ensuring they adhere to relevant laws and guidelines. This can be particularly valuable in areas like financial compliance, data protection, and monitoring for unethical AI use.

Preparing for Future Regulatory Needs

As AI continues to advance, regulations will need to evolve to address new challenges and scenarios. This requires ongoing dialogue between technologists, lawmakers, and other stakeholders. Preparing for future regulatory needs involves anticipating potential AI developments and their societal impacts, and proactively creating frameworks to manage them.

Conclusion

Regulations and compliance in the digital era, particularly concerning advanced language models and AI, are complex and evolving areas. Effective regulation is crucial to ensure that AI technologies are used responsibly and ethically, while also fostering innovation and growth. Balancing these needs requires a multifaceted approach, involving updated laws, ethical guidelines, international cooperation, and the use of AI itself as a tool for compliance. As we continue to integrate AI into various aspects of life, the importance of robust and adaptive regulatory frameworks becomes increasingly apparent.

Chapter 4: Mitigating Risks

Strategies for Secure Deployment of AI Tools

In an era where artificial intelligence (AI) is increasingly integrated into various aspects of life and business, the secure deployment of AI tools, especially advanced language models, has become paramount. Ensuring the security of these AI systems involves a comprehensive approach that addresses potential vulnerabilities and risks. This section outlines key strategies for the secure deployment of AI tools.

Understanding the Security Landscape

Before deploying AI tools, it is essential to understand the specific security risks associated with these technologies. This includes vulnerabilities inherent in AI algorithms, potential data breaches, and the risk of malicious use of AI capabilities. A thorough risk assessment should be conducted to identify and evaluate these risks in the context of the intended deployment environment.

Robust Data Management Practices

Secure deployment of AI starts with robust data management. This involves ensuring the integrity and security of the data used to train and operate AI models. Data encryption, access controls, and regular audits are critical components of data security. Additionally, it's important to adhere to data privacy regulations and ensure that data is collected and used ethically and responsibly.

Secure Development Lifecycle

Integrating security into the development lifecycle of AI tools is vital. This includes implementing secure coding practices, conducting regular security testing throughout the development process, and ensuring that security considerations are integrated into every stage of AI development, from design to deployment.

Monitoring and Maintenance

Ongoing monitoring and maintenance are crucial for the secure deployment of AI tools. This involves regularly updating AI models and systems to address new threats and vulnerabilities, monitoring AI system performance for signs of security breaches or failures, and continuously evaluating the effectiveness of security measures.

AI-Specific Security Measures

Certain security measures are specific to AI systems, particularly those involving machine learning and language models. This includes techniques to protect against adversarial attacks, where small changes to input data can lead to incorrect outputs, and ensuring that AI models are robust against such manipulations.

Training and Awareness

Employees and users of AI tools should be trained in security best practices and made aware of the potential risks associated with AI systems. This includes understanding how to securely interact with AI tools, recognizing potential security threats, and knowing the protocols to follow in the event of a security breach.

Ethical AI Deployment

Secure deployment of AI also involves ethical considerations. This means ensuring that AI tools are used in a manner that respects user privacy, avoids bias and discrimination, and aligns with ethical standards. Developing a set of ethical guidelines for AI deployment can help in navigating these challenges.

Collaboration and Sharing of Best Practices

Collaboration between organizations, cybersecurity experts, and regulatory bodies is essential in developing and sharing best practices for AI security. This can include sharing knowledge about emerging threats, developing common standards for AI security, and working together to enhance the overall security of AI systems.

Legal Compliance and Regulations

Adhering to legal requirements and industry regulations is a critical aspect of secure AI deployment. Organizations should ensure that their use of AI tools complies with relevant laws and regulations, particularly those related to data protection, privacy, and cybersecurity.

Preparing for the Future

Finally, preparing for future security challenges is essential in the rapidly evolving field of AI. This involves staying informed about the latest developments in AI and cybersecurity, anticipating future trends and risks, and being adaptable in updating security strategies as the AI landscape evolves.

Conclusion

The secure deployment of AI tools requires a multi-faceted approach that encompasses robust data management, secure development practices, ongoing monitoring, ethical considerations, and legal compliance. By implementing these strategies, organizations can harness the benefits of AI while minimizing security risks, ensuring that these powerful tools are used safely and responsibly.

Industry Best Practices and Standards

In the rapidly evolving field of artificial intelligence (AI), establishing and adhering to industry best practices and standards is crucial for mitigating risks associated with AI tools, especially advanced language models. This section outlines key best practices and standards that have been identified as essential for the responsible deployment of AI technologies.

Emphasizing Ethical AI Development

Ethical AI development is at the forefront of industry best practices. This involves ensuring that AI tools are designed and deployed in a manner that respects human rights, values, and diversity. Ethical considerations include fairness, transparency, accountability, and respect for user privacy. Organizations are encouraged to develop ethical guidelines for AI use and to ensure that their AI systems adhere to these principles.

Data Privacy and Security

Data privacy and security are critical components of AI best practices. This includes securing data against unauthorized access, ensuring data integrity, and protecting sensitive information. Best practices in this area also involve complying with data protection regulations like GDPR and implementing robust data governance frameworks.

Transparency and Explainability

Transparency in AI operations and the explainability of AI decisions are key industry standards. AI systems, particularly those involved in decision-making processes, should be transparent in how they operate and how decisions are made. This is crucial for building trust among users and for accountability.

Regular Auditing and Compliance Checks

Conducting regular audits and compliance checks is a standard practice in the AI industry. This involves evaluating AI systems for security vulnerabilities, biases, and ethical concerns. Regular auditing helps in identifying potential issues early and in ensuring ongoing compliance with legal and ethical standards.

Ongoing Monitoring and Maintenance

AI systems require ongoing monitoring and maintenance to ensure their continued effectiveness and security. This includes updating AI models to adapt to new data and evolving scenarios, monitoring for any misuse of AI tools, and maintaining the overall health of the AI system.

Collaboration and Knowledge Sharing

Collaboration and knowledge sharing within the AI community are vital for advancing industry best practices. This involves sharing experiences, challenges, and solutions related to AI deployment, and learning from the successes and failures of others. Industry conferences, workshops, and publications are key platforms for this exchange of knowledge.

Risk Assessment and Management

Risk assessment and management are integral to AI deployment. Organizations should conduct thorough risk assessments to identify potential risks associated with their AI tools and implement strategies to manage these risks. This includes considering the impact of AI decisions and preparing contingency plans for potential failures or breaches.

User Education and Awareness

Educating users about the capabilities and limitations of AI tools is an important industry practice. Users should be aware of how AI systems work, the data they use, and the potential risks involved. User education helps in ensuring the responsible use of AI tools and in minimizing misunderstandings and misuse.

Developing AI-specific Security Measures

Given the unique challenges posed by AI, developing AI-specific security measures is essential. This includes protecting against adversarial attacks, securing AI algorithms, and ensuring the robustness of AI systems against manipulation and exploitation.

Adherence to International Standards

Finally, adherence to international standards and guidelines for AI is a key best practice. Organizations should stay informed about international developments in AI regulation and standards, and ensure that their AI deployments are in line with these guidelines. This is particularly important for organizations operating in multiple countries or regions.

Conclusion

Adhering to industry best practices and standards is essential for the secure and responsible deployment of AI tools. These practices encompass ethical AI development, data privacy, transparency, regular auditing, ongoing monitoring, collaboration, risk management, user education, AI-specific security measures, and international compliance. By following these guidelines, organizations can mitigate the risks associated with AI tools and harness their benefits in a responsible and sustainable manner.

Future-Proofing Against AI Vulnerabilities

As artificial intelligence (AI), especially language models, becomes increasingly embedded in various aspects of society and industry, the need to future-proof these systems against vulnerabilities is paramount. This section explores the strategies and approaches necessary to safeguard AI systems from future risks and challenges.

Anticipating Emerging Threats

The first step in future-proofing AI systems is to anticipate and understand potential future threats. This involves staying informed about the latest developments in AI technology and cybersecurity. By understanding potential future vulnerabilities, developers and users of AI systems can proactively implement measures to mitigate these risks.

Continuous Learning and Adaptation

AI systems, particularly those based on machine learning, must be capable of continuous learning and adaptation. This is crucial for them to stay effective in the face of evolving data environments and emerging threats. Continuous learning enables AI systems to adapt to new patterns and behaviors, thereby maintaining their relevance and security.

Robust and Resilient AI Design

Designing AI systems that are robust and resilient to attacks is a critical aspect of future-proofing. This involves developing systems that can withstand adversarial attacks, errors, and unexpected inputs without significant degradation in performance. Techniques such as adversarial training, where AI systems are exposed to potential attack scenarios during development, can enhance their robustness.

Ethical and Responsible AI Development

Future-proofing AI also involves ethical and responsible development. As AI systems become more advanced, ensuring that they are developed with ethical considerations in mind is crucial. This includes addressing issues of bias, fairness, transparency, and accountability.

Regular Security Audits and Updates

Conducting regular security audits and updates is essential for the long-term security of AI systems. Regular audits help identify new vulnerabilities and areas where the AI system may be lacking. Keeping AI systems updated with the latest security patches and improvements is crucial in protecting them against known threats.

Data Governance and Privacy Measures

Strong data governance and privacy measures are fundamental in future-proofing AI systems. As data is the lifeblood of most AI systems, ensuring its integrity, confidentiality, and availability is paramount. This involves implementing strong data encryption, access controls, and privacy-preserving techniques like anonymization.

Developing AI-Specific Security Standards

The development of AI-specific security standards and best practices is a key strategy in future-proofing. These standards can provide guidelines for AI development, deployment, and maintenance, helping ensure that AI systems are secure and reliable.

Fostering a Culture of Security Awareness

Creating a culture of security awareness among developers, users, and stakeholders of AI systems is crucial. Educating people about the potential risks and best practices in AI security can lead to more vigilant and responsible use and development of AI technologies.

Collaboration and Information Sharing

Collaboration and information sharing among AI developers, researchers, and cybersecurity experts are essential in identifying and mitigating future threats. Sharing knowledge about vulnerabilities, attack techniques, and defense strategies can help strengthen the security of all AI systems.

Preparing for Regulatory Changes

Staying prepared for potential regulatory changes is also important in future-proofing AI systems. As AI technology evolves, so too will the regulatory landscape. Being adaptable and ready to comply with new regulations ensures that AI systems remain viable and legal.

Conclusion

Future-proofing against AI vulnerabilities requires a multifaceted approach involving continuous learning, robust design, ethical development, regular audits, strong data governance, AI-specific security standards, security awareness, collaboration, and preparedness for regulatory changes. By adopting these strategies, AI systems, especially advanced language models, can be safeguarded against emerging threats, ensuring their long-term viability and security.

Chapter 5:
The Future of AI in Language and Security

Emerging Trends in AI and Language Processing

The field of artificial intelligence (AI), especially in language processing, is evolving rapidly, with new trends and developments emerging constantly. Understanding these trends is crucial for anticipating future directions and implications of AI in various sectors. This section explores the latest trends in AI and language processing.

Advancements in Natural Language Understanding (NLU)

One of the most significant trends in AI language processing is the continued advancement in Natural Language Understanding (NLU). NLU technologies have moved beyond basic text interpretation to more sophisticated understanding of context, sentiment, and nuances in language. This advancement allows AI systems to engage in more complex and meaningful interactions, opening new possibilities in areas like conversational AI, content analysis, and human-computer interaction.

Integration of Multimodal AI

The integration of multimodal AI, which combines text, voice, images, and other data types, is an emerging trend. This holistic approach enhances the AI's understanding by providing a more comprehensive view of user interactions. In language processing, this means AI can interpret not just the words but also the accompanying visual or auditory cues, leading to more accurate and contextual responses.

AI-Driven Personalization

Another key trend is the increased use of AI for personalization. Language models are being used to tailor content, recommendations, and interactions to individual preferences and behaviors. This personalization is evident in marketing, content delivery platforms, and personalized education tools, where AI adapts to individual user needs and preferences.

Expansion of AI in Non-English Languages

There is a growing emphasis on expanding AI capabilities in non-English languages. Historically, AI language models have focused predominantly on English, but there is an increasing effort to develop models that are inclusive of a wider range of languages and dialects. This trend is crucial for making AI accessible and useful to a global audience.

Ethical AI and Bias Mitigation

The trend towards ethical AI and bias mitigation is gaining momentum. As the impact of AI on society becomes more evident, there is a growing focus on developing AI in a responsible manner. This includes efforts to identify and mitigate biases in AI models, ensuring that AI systems are fair, transparent, and accountable.

AI for Accessibility

Using AI to enhance accessibility is an emerging trend. Language models are being developed to assist individuals with disabilities, such as real-time translation for the hearing impaired or text-to-speech for the visually impaired. This trend reflects a broader move towards using AI to create more inclusive technologies.

AI in Cybersecurity

In the realm of security, the use of AI for threat detection and response is an important trend. Language processing AI is being employed to analyze communications and detect phishing attempts, fraud, and other cybersecurity threats. This trend is crucial as cyber threats become more sophisticated and prevalent.

Edge AI and Language Processing

The emergence of edge AI, where AI processing is done on local devices instead of in the cloud, is a notable trend in language processing. This approach offers benefits in terms of speed, privacy, and connectivity. Edge AI is particularly relevant in applications like voice assistants and real-time translation devices.

The Convergence of AI and IoT

The convergence of AI with the Internet of Things (IoT) is a trend with significant implications for language processing. AI-enabled IoT devices can use language processing to interpret and respond to voice commands, interact with users, and provide personalized experiences.

Preparing for Quantum AI

Finally, the preparation for quantum AI represents a forward-looking trend. While still in its early stages, the potential of quantum computing to revolutionize AI, including language processing, is immense. Quantum AI could lead to significant breakthroughs in processing speed and AI capabilities.

Conclusion

The emerging trends in AI and language processing indicate a future where AI is more sophisticated, inclusive, ethical, and integrated into various aspects of life and business. From advancements in NLU to the convergence of AI with IoT, these trends point to a rapidly evolving landscape. As AI continues to advance, staying informed and adaptable will be key for organizations and individuals looking to leverage AI technologies effectively.

Predictions for the Next Decade

As we stand at the forefront of AI innovation, particularly in language processing and security, predicting the trajectory of these technologies over the next decade is both fascinating and crucial. This section presents a series of predictions about the future of AI in these fields, drawing on current trends and emerging technologies.

Advancements in Language Model Capabilities

1. **Near-Human Level Language Understanding**: In the next decade, AI language models are predicted to achieve near-human levels of understanding and generating text. This would mean a greater ability to comprehend context, sarcasm, and complex language nuances, making AI much more effective in natural language interactions.

2. **Personalized AI Assistants**: We can expect the emergence of highly personalized AI assistants that can understand and predict individual preferences and needs, offering a level of personalization that goes beyond current capabilities.

Breakthroughs in Multimodal AI

1. **Seamless Integration of Text, Voice, and Visual Data**: AI systems will likely integrate text, voice, and visual data more seamlessly, allowing for more comprehensive and contextual interactions. This could revolutionize areas like virtual reality, augmented reality, and interactive learning.

2. **Enhanced Human-AI Collaboration**: The next decade should see AI systems becoming more of a collaborative partner, capable of understanding and participating in creative and problem-solving processes alongside humans.

AI in Cybersecurity

1. **Proactive Threat Detection and Response**: AI systems are expected to become more proactive in detecting and responding to cybersecurity threats, using predictive analytics to anticipate and neutralize threats before they materialize.

2. **AI in Cyber Warfare**: Unfortunately, the use of AI in cyber warfare is likely to increase, with nation-states and organizations using AI-powered tools for both defensive and offensive cyber operations.

Ethical AI Development

1. **Stronger Focus on Ethical AI**: As AI becomes more integrated into society, a stronger focus on ethical AI development is expected. This includes more robust frameworks and guidelines to ensure AI is developed and used responsibly.

2. **Global AI Governance**: The next decade might see the establishment of global AI governance bodies, aimed at setting international standards and regulations for AI development and use.

AI Accessibility and Inclusivity

1. **AI for Global Language Inclusivity**: AI developments are likely to focus on inclusivity, with language models supporting a wider range of languages and dialects, thus democratizing access to technology.

2. **AI for Accessibility**: Enhanced AI tools are expected to play a significant role in accessibility, providing advanced solutions for individuals with disabilities, such as sophisticated AI-driven aids for the visually or hearing-impaired.

Quantum Computing and AI

1. **Quantum-AI Integration:** The integration of quantum computing and AI could lead to breakthroughs in processing capabilities, enabling AI systems to solve complex problems much faster than current systems.

2. **Quantum-Enhanced Machine Learning:** Machine learning models could be significantly enhanced by quantum computing, leading to faster learning times and the ability to process extraordinarily large datasets.

AI in Education and Workforce

1. **Personalized Learning:** AI is predicted to revolutionize education with highly personalized learning experiences, adapting to individual learning styles and needs.

2. **AI Literacy in Workforce:** As AI becomes more prevalent, AI literacy will become a critical skill in the workforce, with more emphasis on training workers to collaborate effectively with AI systems.

Challenges and Opportunities

1. **Balancing AI Advancements with Ethical Considerations:** One of the biggest challenges will be balancing rapid AI advancements with ethical considerations and societal impacts.

2. **Addressing AI and Employment:** There will be a need to address the impact of AI on employment, including re-skilling and up-skilling of the workforce.

Conclusion

The next decade in AI, particularly in language processing and security, is poised to bring groundbreaking advancements and transformative changes. While these predictions paint an exciting picture of AI's potential, they also underscore the need for careful consideration of ethical, societal, and security implications. The future of AI will likely be characterized by remarkable innovation, but also by the imperative to navigate these developments responsibly and equitably.

Preparing for a Secure AI-Driven Future

The rapid advancement of AI, especially in language processing and security, is reshaping our future. Preparing for an AI-driven future involves not just embracing these technological advancements but also ensuring that they are developed and used securely and ethically. This section explores the key strategies and considerations for preparing for a secure AI-driven future.

Emphasizing Ethical AI Development

1. **Establishing Ethical Guidelines**: The foundation for a secure AI-driven future is the establishment of strong ethical guidelines for AI development and use. These guidelines should emphasize fairness, transparency, accountability, and respect for privacy.

2. **Incorporating Ethics in AI Education**: Ethical considerations should be an integral part of AI education and training programs. This will help inculcate a sense of responsibility among future AI developers and users.

Advancing Cybersecurity Measures

1. **Staying Ahead of AI-Driven Threats**: As AI becomes more sophisticated, so do the threats it poses. Advancing cybersecurity measures to stay ahead of these threats is crucial. This involves not only technological solutions but also strategic planning and policy-making.

2. **Developing AI-Resilient Security Systems**: There is a need to develop security systems that are resilient to AI-driven attacks. This includes using AI itself to detect and counteract AI-generated threats.

Fostering Public Awareness and Engagement

1. **Educating the Public**: Public awareness and understanding of AI technologies, their benefits, and risks are essential. Educational initiatives should aim to demystify AI and promote informed discussions about its impact.

2. **Encouraging Public Participation**: Public participation in discussions about AI development and policy-making should be encouraged. This helps in ensuring that AI technologies align with societal values and needs.

Prioritizing Data Privacy and Protection

1. **Robust Data Governance**: Strong data governance policies are essential in an AI-driven future. This includes secure data handling practices, ensuring data privacy, and complying with data protection regulations.

2. **Empowering Individuals Regarding Their Data**: Individuals should have control over their data, including understanding how it is used and the ability to opt-out of data collection where necessary.

Investing in AI Research and Development

1. **Focus on Beneficial AI**: Investment in AI research and development should focus on areas that offer significant benefits to society, such as healthcare, education, and environmental protection.

2. **Supporting Interdisciplinary Research**: AI research should be interdisciplinary, combining insights from technology, social sciences, ethics, and law to create well-rounded AI solutions.

Building Collaborative Ecosystems

1. **Promoting Collaboration**: Collaboration between governments, industry, academia, and civil society is key to preparing for an AI-driven future. This collaborative approach can lead to more holistic and effective AI solutions.

2. **Global Cooperation**: Given the global nature of AI, international cooperation is crucial. This includes sharing best practices, research, and policies to ensure a harmonized approach to AI development and governance.

Preparing the Workforce

1. **Reskilling and Upskilling**: As AI transforms industries, reskilling and upskilling the workforce become necessary. Training programs should focus on AI literacy and skills to work alongside AI technologies.

2. **Creating New Job Opportunities**: While AI may automate certain jobs, it also creates new opportunities. Identifying and fostering these new roles is essential for a smooth transition to an AI-driven economy.

Ethical Use of AI in Governance

1. **AI in Public Services**: AI can significantly enhance public services and governance. However, its use must be transparent, accountable, and aligned with public interest.

2. **Regulatory Oversight**: Adequate regulatory oversight is necessary to ensure that AI is used responsibly in governance. This includes regular audits and adherence to ethical standards.

Conclusion

Preparing for a secure AI-driven future requires a multifaceted approach. It involves not only advancing technology but also fostering ethical development, enhancing cybersecurity, raising public awareness, prioritizing data privacy, investing in research, building collaborative ecosystems, preparing the workforce, and ensuring ethical use in governance. By addressing these areas, we can steer the course of AI towards a future that is secure, ethical, and beneficial for all.

Conclusion: Navigating a Secure Path Forward

Summarizing Key Insights

The exploration of language models in the realm of AI and their impact on security, as detailed in "The Future of Words: Security in the Age of Advanced Language Models," reveals a landscape filled with opportunities, challenges, and responsibilities. The key insights summarized here are pivotal in understanding the book's comprehensive analysis of this complex and dynamic field.

The Evolution and Capabilities of Language Models

The book begins by tracing the evolution of language technology, from its early rule-based systems to today's advanced language models like GPT. These models, powered by deep learning and neural networks, demonstrate remarkable capabilities in understanding, processing, and generating human language. They have transcended basic text interpretation to include context, emotion, and even cultural nuances, marking a significant leap in AI's interaction with human language.

The Impact on Society and Industry

Language models have undeniably transformed various sectors including customer service, content creation, education, and healthcare. They have democratized access to information, personalized user experiences, and streamlined business processes. However, this transformation is not without its challenges. The book highlights the importance of balancing these advancements with the potential risks and ethical considerations.

Security Landscapes and Language Models

A focal point of the book is the intricate relationship between language models and cybersecurity. The use of AI in enhancing security systems, through threat detection and response, is counterbalanced by the risks these models pose, including their potential use in sophisticated cyberattacks like phishing and social engineering. The dual nature of AI in cybersecurity underscores the need for robust, AI-informed security strategies.

Ethical Considerations and Regulatory Challenges

The book emphasizes the ethical implications of language models. Issues such as data privacy, algorithmic bias, and the potential for misuse are critical considerations. The discussion extends to the need for clear regulatory frameworks and policies that keep pace with technological advancements, ensuring responsible and ethical use of AI.

Strategies for Risk Mitigation

Mitigating risks associated with language models is another key insight. The book outlines strategies such as developing ethical AI guidelines, implementing strong data governance, and conducting regular security audits. It also stresses the importance of user education and awareness as crucial components in mitigating risks.

The Role of Collaboration and Global Governance

The global nature of AI technology necessitates international collaboration and governance. The book advocates for a unified approach to AI development and regulation, emphasizing the need for international standards and cooperation to address the challenges posed by AI.

Future Trends and Preparations

Looking ahead, the book predicts significant advancements in AI and language processing. These include the development of more sophisticated, multimodal AI systems and the integration of AI in various sectors. Preparing for these advancements involves continuous learning, adaptation, and anticipation of future challenges, particularly in the realms of cybersecurity and ethical AI development.

Balancing Innovation with Societal Needs

A recurring theme in the book is the need to balance technological innovation with societal needs and ethical considerations. As AI continues to evolve, ensuring that its development and deployment benefit society as a whole remains a paramount concern.

Navigating the AI-Driven Future

In conclusion, the book presents a comprehensive overview of the current state and future potential of language models in AI, emphasizing the need for a balanced, informed, and proactive approach. The insights gathered underscore the importance of responsible innovation, ethical considerations, security awareness, and international cooperation in navigating the AI-driven future.

Recommendations for Policymakers and Technologists

In the landscape of advanced language models and AI, the roles of policymakers and technologists are pivotal. Their decisions and innovations shape how these technologies evolve and integrate into society. This section outlines key recommendations for both groups, aiming to foster a responsible, secure, and beneficial development and deployment of AI.

For Policymakers

1. **Develop Comprehensive AI Policies**: Policymakers should develop comprehensive AI policies that address ethical, privacy, and security aspects of AI. These policies need to be adaptable to the fast-paced evolution of AI technologies.

2. **Promote AI Literacy and Public Engagement**: Implementing programs to enhance AI literacy among the public and encouraging engagement in AI policy discussions can lead

to more informed decision-making and a population that is better prepared for an AI-driven future.

3. **Foster International Collaboration**: AI technologies transcend borders, so international collaboration in AI policy and regulation is crucial. Policymakers should work towards global standards and agreements to address challenges like data privacy, security, and ethical AI use.

4. **Support AI Research and Innovation**: Policymakers should promote and support research in AI, focusing on beneficial and ethical applications. Funding and resources should be allocated to areas of AI that promise significant social benefits.

5. **Ensure AI Inclusivity and Accessibility**: Policies should ensure that AI technologies are inclusive and accessible to all, regardless of socioeconomic background, language, or disability. This includes supporting AI development in diverse languages and for varied user needs.

For Technologists

1. **Prioritize Ethical AI Development**: Technologists must prioritize ethical considerations in AI development. This includes building AI systems that are fair, transparent, accountable, and free from biases, and respecting user privacy and data security.

2. **Engage in Interdisciplinary Collaboration**: AI development should not be siloed in the technical domain. Engaging with experts in ethics, sociology, law, and other disciplines can provide a holistic approach to AI development.

3. **Implement Robust Security Measures**: Given the increasing use of AI in critical and sensitive areas, technologists should implement robust security measures to protect AI systems from vulnerabilities and malicious use.

4. **Focus on User-Centric Design:** AI technologies should be designed with the end-user in mind. This involves understanding and addressing user needs, concerns, and feedback, and ensuring that AI systems are user-friendly and accessible.

5. **Continuously Update and Educate:** The fast-evolving nature of AI demands continuous learning and adaptation. Technologists should stay updated with the latest developments and trends in AI and contribute to the education of the next generation of AI professionals.

Collaborative Efforts

1. **Joint Task Forces and Committees:** Policymakers and technologists should form joint task forces or committees to address specific AI challenges, ensuring that policies and technological developments are aligned and mutually beneficial.

2. **Public-Private Partnerships:** Encouraging public-private partnerships can lead to more effective and efficient development and deployment of AI technologies, leveraging the strengths of both sectors.

3. **Community Engagement and Feedback:** Engaging with communities and obtaining feedback can help policymakers and technologists understand the real-world impact of AI and adjust their approaches accordingly.

Conclusion

In conclusion, the collaboration between policymakers and technologists is essential in steering the development and use of AI and language models towards a future that is secure, ethical, and beneficial for society. Policymakers must craft thoughtful, inclusive policies, while technologists should focus on ethical, user-centric, and secure AI development. Together, their coordinated efforts can harness the transformative potential of AI while addressing its challenges.

Envisioning the Future of AI in Language and Security

As we stand at the precipice of a new era in technology, envisioning the future of AI in the realms of language and security involves both excitement and caution. This section explores potential future developments and their implications, drawing upon the insights and trends discussed throughout "The Future of Words: Security in the Age of Advanced Language Models."

Advanced Language Models and Communication

1. **Seamless Human-AI Interaction**: The future may see language models achieving near-perfect fluency in human communication, enabling seamless interactions between humans and AI. This could revolutionize customer service, education, and entertainment, providing more personalized and efficient experiences.

2. **Breaking Language Barriers**: Advanced translation capabilities of AI could lead to the breaking down of language barriers, fostering global communication and understanding. We might witness a world where language differences are no longer a hurdle in global collaboration and cultural exchange.

AI in Creative and Cognitive Tasks

1. **AI as a Creative Partner**: AI's role in creative processes is expected to expand, with AI assisting in writing, art, and design. This collaboration could lead to new forms of art and literature, though it also raises questions about creativity and originality.

2. **Cognitive Enhancement**: AI might play a role in enhancing human cognitive capabilities, assisting in complex problem-solving, learning, and decision-making processes. This could have significant implications for education and professional fields.

Security Applications and Challenges

1. **Proactive Security Measures**: AI is likely to be increasingly used in proactive security measures, predicting and mitigating risks before they manifest. This could include advanced threat detection systems in cybersecurity and predictive policing in law enforcement.

2. **Ethical and Privacy Concerns**: With the increasing use of AI in security, ethical and privacy concerns will become more pronounced. Balancing security benefits with individual rights will be a critical challenge.

The Evolution of Cyber Threats

1. **AI-Driven Cyberattacks**: The future might witness more sophisticated cyberattacks powered by AI, including the use of AI in creating malware and conducting large-scale, targeted phishing campaigns.

2. **AI in Cyber Defense**: Conversely, AI will also play a crucial role in cyber defense, with automated systems detecting and responding to threats faster and more effectively than ever before.

Regulatory and Ethical Considerations

1. **Evolving Regulations**: As AI becomes more entrenched in society, regulatory frameworks will need to evolve to address the new challenges and realities of AI technology, especially in terms of privacy, security, and ethical use.

2. **Global AI Ethics Standards**: There may be a push towards establishing global ethics standards for AI development and deployment, ensuring that AI is used for the benefit of humanity while minimizing potential harms.

Social and Economic Impacts

1. **Impact on Employment**: AI's impact on employment will continue to be a significant issue, with the potential for both job displacement and the creation of new job categories. Adapting to this changing job landscape will be crucial.

2. **AI and Inequality**: There is a risk that AI could exacerbate social and economic inequalities if not managed carefully. Ensuring equitable access to AI benefits will be a vital consideration.

Conclusion

The future of AI in language and security presents a landscape replete with possibilities and challenges. From revolutionizing communication to reshaping security paradigms, the potential of AI is immense. However, this future also demands responsible stewardship, ethical considerations, and proactive measures to ensure that the benefits of AI are realized while minimizing its risks. As we move forward, it is crucial that we navigate this future with a balanced approach, fostering innovation while safeguarding ethical values and security.

Final Thoughts and Recommendations

As we conclude our exploration in "The Future of Words: Security in the Age of Advanced Language Models," it is evident that the intersection of AI, language, and security is not just a technological concern but a societal one. The book has traversed various dimensions of this intersection, from the evolution of language models to their implications for security, ethics, and society. Here, we consolidate our insights and put forth recommendations for a future that harnesses AI's potential responsibly and ethically.

Embracing AI with Awareness and Responsibility

1. **Conscious Development and Deployment**: AI should be developed and deployed with a conscious understanding of its potential impacts. This requires a commitment from technol-

ogists and policymakers to prioritize ethical considerations and societal well-being alongside innovation.

2. **Promoting Transparency and Accountability**: Transparency in AI operations and accountability for their outcomes are essential. Users and impacted parties should have a clear understanding of how AI systems operate and the principles guiding their functioning.

Strengthening Security and Ethical Frameworks

1. **Robust Security Measures**: As AI becomes increasingly integrated into our digital infrastructure, robust security measures to protect against AI-driven threats are crucial. This includes ongoing risk assessments and the development of AI-specific security protocols.

2. **Ethical AI Governance**: Establishing comprehensive ethical frameworks for AI development and use is imperative. This should include guidelines for fairness, non-discrimination, privacy, and ensuring that AI benefits are equitably distributed.

Fostering Informed Public Engagement

1. **Educating and Engaging the Public**: Public education on AI's capabilities, risks, and ethical implications is crucial. An informed public can better engage in discourse and decision-making regarding AI's role in society.

2. **Inclusive Policymaking**: AI policymaking should be inclusive, reflecting diverse perspectives and needs. Public participation in AI governance can help ensure that policies are balanced and equitable.

Preparing for the Future Workforce

1. **Reskilling and Upskilling Initiatives**: As AI transforms the job landscape, reskilling and upskilling initiatives become vital. These programs should focus on imparting AI literacy and skills necessary to thrive in an AI-integrated future.

2. **Creating New Opportunities**: It's important to explore and create new job opportunities that AI advancements may bring. This proactive approach can help mitigate the employment challenges posed by AI automation.

International Collaboration and Regulation

1. **Global Cooperation**: AI's implications transcend national boundaries, necessitating international collaboration in developing AI policies, standards, and regulatory frameworks.

2. **Harmonizing AI Regulations**: Efforts should be made to harmonize AI regulations across different regions to ensure consistency in AI development and deployment while respecting local contexts and needs.

Leveraging AI for Societal Benefits

1. **AI for Social Good**: AI should be leveraged to address key societal challenges, such as healthcare, education, and environmental sustainability. This focus can maximize AI's potential for social good.

2. **Accessibility and Inclusion**: AI development should prioritize accessibility and inclusivity, ensuring that AI tools are available and useful to all segments of society, including marginalized groups.

Continuous Research and Adaptation

1. **Ongoing AI Research**: Continuous research into AI's evolving capabilities, impacts, and ethical considerations is essential to stay ahead of emerging challenges and opportunities.

2. **Adaptive Policies and Practices**: Policies and practices surrounding AI should be adaptive, evolving in response to new developments and insights in the field.

Conclusion

"The Future of Words: Security in the Age of Advanced Language Models" underscores the transformative potential of AI in language and security. However, this transformation brings with it a responsibility to navigate these advancements thoughtfully. By embracing AI with awareness, strengthening ethical and security frameworks, fostering public engagement, preparing for workforce changes, collaborating internationally, leveraging AI for societal benefits, and committing to ongoing research and adaptation, we can steer the AI-driven future towards a trajectory that is secure, ethical, and beneficial for all.